Planets

A LEGO® ADVENTURE IN THE REAL WORLD

By Penelope Arlon and
Tory Gordon-Harris

> 3, 2, 1 . . . BLAST OFF! Let's zoom into space and discover new worlds!

📖 SCHOLASTIC

New York   Toronto   London   Auckland
Sydney   Mexico City   New Delhi   Hong Kong

Welcome, LEGO fans!

LEGO® Minifigures show you the world in a unique non-fiction programme.

This book is part of a programme of LEGO® non-fiction books, with something for all the family, at every age and stage. LEGO non-fiction books have amazing facts, beautiful real-world photos, and minifigures everywhere, leading the fun and discovery.

To find out about the books in the programme, visit www.scholastic.co.uk.

FSC
www.fsc.org

MIX
Paper from responsible sources
FSC® C012700

Scholastic Children's Books
Euston House,
24 Eversholt Street,
London NW1 1DB, UK
A division of Scholastic Ltd
London ~ New York ~ Toronto ~ Sydney ~ Auckland
Mexico City ~ New Delhi ~ Hong Kong

This book was first published in the US in 2016 by Scholastic Inc.
Published in the UK by Scholastic Ltd, 2016

ISBN 978 1407 16435 9

2 4 6 8 10 9 7 5 3 1

Printed in Malaysia.

There's so much to explore in space. Come and find me!

Contents

Build it!
There are plenty of ideas for builds that are out of this world as you zoom through this book!

Play it!
Look out for these great ideas for minifigure action. Create space adventures of your own!

I can't wait for you to join me. I could use some company!

I can't wait for my first space adventure to Mars!

Planet spotting

For thousands of years, people spotted planets in the night sky. Now incredible machines help us see into deep space – and some even travel there!

Mercury, Venus, Mars, Jupiter, and Saturn can be spotted from your own backyard. Just lie down and look up!

Stare hard enough, and you may spot me out there!

Space telescopes can see billions of miles away. But we still want to see further . . .

Telescopes
The five closest planets can be seen in the night sky with just binoculars or a telescope.

Giant telescopes
All over the world, huge telescopes spot faraway planets in distant space.

Space telescopes
Telescopes can see better when they are away from Earth, so we send them into space!

Rockets

Everything that travels to space has to be blasted off Earth in rockets. That includes machines and people.

Space probes do not have people on them. Send ME out to explore!

Woo-hoo! We're off!

Build it!

Build a space probe that can discover new worlds. Here are some famous space probes.

Galileo

Magellan

Stardust

Rosetta

Juno

LRO

Build it bigger!

Probes have huge panels, like wings, that unfold to catch the sunlight. Build two on your space probe.

Space probes

These small machines travel through space, sending back information and photos.

Humans

We've been to the Moon, and soon we'll be visiting Mars, too!

The Sun

The Sun, which lights and heats our planet, is our very own star. It's a super-hot ball of fiery gas and is REALLY, REALLY big.

SOLAR PROBE PLUS

Starting in 2018, this space probe will fly around the Sun 24 times, sending red-hot info back to Earth.

Superstar

About 1 million Earths could fit inside the Sun! The Sun's centre is 15 million°C. It's so hot that space probes (and spaceships) melt if they get too close.

Scientists have recorded strange tunes coming out of the Sun. Want to hear some hot rock?

Gulp! Can't we hear it on a radio?

HOT FACT

A piece of the Sun's centre the size of a pinhead would be so hot it would be deadly to people 100 miles (161 km) away!

Build it!
Build a spacecraft that can take the heat!

MEDIUM STAR
Our Sun is only a medium-sized star. There are some stars in space that are 100 times bigger!

Ah! The Sun is a real star, just like me. There aren't very many REAL stars out there.

Actually, there are about 1 billion trillion other stars out there . . .

9

Our solar system

Our Sun is at the centre of a family of planets and rocks called the solar system. Eight planets and millions of rocks all move around the Sun in circles, called orbits.

Venus

Earth

Mercury

Mars

Rocky planets
The first four planets, nearest the Sun, are made of rock. They are the smallest planets.

Gas giants
The four planets furthest from the Sun are made of gas. The gas planets are COLOSSAL!

JUPITER

Jupiter is the largest of all our Sun's planets.

Everything moves around the Sun because of GRAVITY. The Sun is a bit like a magnet, pulling everything towards it. Nothing floats away. That's gravity.

Far out, man!

Space rocks

In between Mars and Jupiter are billions of rocks. These rocks are known as the asteroid belt. They travel around the Sun, too. Beyond Neptune are more icy rocks, and maybe even a giant ninth planet, called Planet X.

SATURN
Huge rocky rings surround Saturn.

URANUS
Uranus is very cold and very dark.

NEPTUNE
Neptune is the furthest planet from the Sun.

Earth also has gravity, which keeps us from floating away. Mars has less gravity than Earth does.

And jump high, too! Let's hold the next Olympics on Mars . . .

So that means that we can lift really heavy things on Mars. AWESOME!

Mercury

If you travel outwards from the Sun, the first planet you get to is the smallest and speediest, Mercury.
It is super-hot! Hotter than your oven at full heat. Ouch!

Mercury

MESSENGER

The NASA space probe *MESSENGER* took six-and-a half years to reach Mercury. It was tricky to catch up with it because the planet moves so fast! In 2011, *MESSENGER* took the first good pictures of Mercury.

An atmosphere is a thick layer of gases that surrounds some planets, including ours. It protects the planet, like a blanket. Mercury has no atmosphere.

SUN POWER

Solar panels on the probe made electricity from sunlight. They powered the probe through space.

PLANET STATS

- Made of: Rock and metal
- Moons: 0
- Rings: 0
- Distance from Sun:
  40 million miles
  (58 million km)
- Space-probe missions: 2

BAM SLAM

With no atmosphere, Mercury gets smashed by space rocks!

Mercury is the smallest planet in our solar system, right?

Smash!

Mercury's ground is full of holes, called craters, because of the space rocks that slam into it. It's a dangerous place to be!

Yes! And it's set to hold that record. Mercury is shrinking! Just like this hot dog! Yum!

Crash!

In 2015, *MESSENGER* flew down to the surface of Mercury. It sent back information as it crashed into the planet and left a crater 15 metres wide!

The second planet from the Sun is Venus. Venus is like Earth's evil twin. It is nearly the same size as Earth and has clouds and weather like Earth does. But unlike Earth, it is very, very poisonous and very, very hot.

Ew, stinky!

Venus has a thick atmosphere, which means that it has weather, like Earth does. But it is ALWAYS cloudy on Venus. Scientists think that the air might smell like rotten eggs – yuck!

MAGELLAN

In the 1990s, the space probe *Magellan* flew near Venus and mapped it for us.

> Venus is named after the Roman god of love.

> Venus sounded romantic, but this is no honeymoon resort.

> They say it's hot enough to melt pla— outside, and the air super poisonous

Steamy hot

When the Sun's heat hits Venus, the clouds trap it in. So it gets hotter and hotter. Even hotter than Mercury!

PLANET STATS

- Made of: Rock
- Moons: 0
- Rings: 0
- Distance from Sun:
  67 million miles
  (108 million km)
- Space-probe missions: 41

MAAT MONS

The highest volcano on Venus is known as Maat Mons. The crater is ENORMOUS!

Ha! Those Earthlings don't seem to be able to survive anywhere.

Let's head for the Moon, Honey!

Our own planet, Earth, is the third planet from the Sun. It is covered in water and is the only planet known to have life. That makes it really special.

Water

Water is the reason why plants and animals can live on Earth. If we can find another planet or moon with water on it, there might be life there, too.

We have better maps of Mars than of our own ocean floor.

Hmm, that's not very helpful . . .

PLANET STATS

- Made of: Rock
- 70% of surface covered in water
- Moons: 1
  - Rings: 0
  - Distance from Sun: 93 million miles (150 million km)
    - Space-probe missions: Exploration happening all the time

Atmosphere

Our planet is surrounded by a thick atmosphere that protects it from flying rocks. It also gives us clouds and weather.

Do you think that aliens look like people?

Well, look at the difference between lions and butterflies. That shows how different from us aliens could be!

ER60082

The Moon

Our Moon is a huge ball of rock that moves around Earth and with us through space. Our Moon is our closest neighbour — but it is still 250,000 miles (402,000 km) from Earth!

MOON SEAS

The dark patches on the Moon are called seas. But they don't have any water in them.

CRATERS

These holes, called craters, show where huge rocks have bashed into the Moon.

What is a moon?

A moon is an object that orbits a planet, held by the planet's gravity. Earth has only one moon, but some other planets have many, many more.

Yawn! Is the Moon made of cheese?

No. The surface of the Moon is rock, covered in a layer of thin dust. Nobody knows what is below the surface, since nobody has dug a big hole yet.

So the inside could be made of cheese?

Moon shapes

The Sun shines only on one side of the Moon. We see different amounts of the lit part as the Moon orbits Earth. That's why the Moon appears to change shape in the sky.

Step on it!

There is no wind on the Moon, so if you make a footprint on it, it will stay for ever. This 40-year-old footprint is still there.

> It would take 133 days to drive non-stop to the Moon. Without a snack break? Seriously?

Man on the Moon

In 1969, Neil Armstrong was the first man to walk on the Moon. He and two other astronauts dropped from their spaceship in a little lander called *Eagle*.

> Sigh . . . Very unlikely.

Moon adventure

DRIVING ON THE MOON

In 1972, astronaut Eugene Cernan drove 21 miles (34 km) on the Moon. This photograph shows Cernan checking over the lunar rover, before loading up and heading out.

PLAY IT!
Take your astronauts to the Moon and help them explore. What will they find?

Only 12 people have ever walked on the Moon. In 1972, Eugene Cernan left Earth on the Apollo 17 mission. He travelled to the Moon and was the last person to walk on it. Nobody has been there since. The exciting thing about the trip was that he took a car with him. He got to drive around in the lunar rover! It couldn't go very fast, because it's pretty rocky on the Moon. But it still holds the record for the fastest-moving land vehicle away from Earth!

Just before heading back to Earth, Cernan wrote his daughter Tracy's initials, TDC, in the dust. They will be there for ever . . . or until the next Moon visitor rubs them out.

Did you know that the lunar rover goes only 8 miles per hour (13 kph)?

Are you kidding me? All that space to race, and I could RUN faster than that!

A baseball would travel faster on the Moon than Earth, as there is no atmosphere to slow it down.

Far out, man . . .

Play it! Here are some ideas . . .

 1 *Do your astronauts have a vehicle?*

 2 *Are there any other visitors to the Moon?*

 3 *Is the Moon made of cheese? Or maybe gold?*

Stargazing

Look into the sky on a clear night – it's full of stars. Thousands of years ago, people joined the stars into shapes that they could recognize, like making join-the-dots drawings. The shapes are called constellations. Learn how to spot some.

You'll impress everyone if you can point this one out!

I'm the dazzling queen of the stars.

Anyone seen my bone?

The Big Dipper
This shape is one of the easiest to spot in the night sky.

Cassiopeia (queen)
This constellation was named after Cassiopeia, a Greek queen.

Canis Major (dog)
Sirius, the brightest star in the sky, is part of this group of stars.

The Milky Way

All the stars that we can see are in our galaxy, the Milky Way. A galaxy is a vast family of stars that move together. Our Sun is one of billions of stars in the Milky Way.

> Rooooarrrr!

> The sky is not the place for fish . . .

> Me see bull in sky . . .

Pisces (fish)

The fish constellation is huge but quite faint.

Taurus (bull)

10,000-year-old cave paintings show the bull.

Draco (dragon)

This dragon wraps itself around the North Star.

Mars

Mars is red. It looks red hot, but it is actually freezing cold because it is further away from the Sun than Earth is. Despite this, astronauts are still racing to get there!

Mars takeover

Mars is the easiest planet for us to send people to. We have already sent robot rovers, like Curiosity, to sniff around for us.

PLANET STATS

- Made of: Rock
- Moons: 2
- Rings: 0
- Distance from Sun: 142 million miles (229 million km)
- Space-probe missions: 44

MINI MOONS

Mars has two tiny moons. Phobos is much smaller than our Moon, and Deimos is even smaller than Phobos.

Hey, I'm here, you know.

Sigh . . . I'm bored. I can't wait for those Earthlings to get here . . .

Wanted: people willing to go to Mars. Here are a few things that you need to know . . .

I'll need some great music!

It's going to be at least a three-year trip.

Okay! Where's the menu?

No fussy eaters. Food is brought from Earth.

I should have had a haircut . . .

There are HUGE dust storms.

Sigh . . . I think I can see America.

Earth is far, far away.

We drink our leftovers?

ALL water is recycled.

No return ticket? Now you tell me, dude!

No one is sure how to get back to Earth.

If you think I'm going to Mars after all that, you must be on another planet!

25

Mars adventure

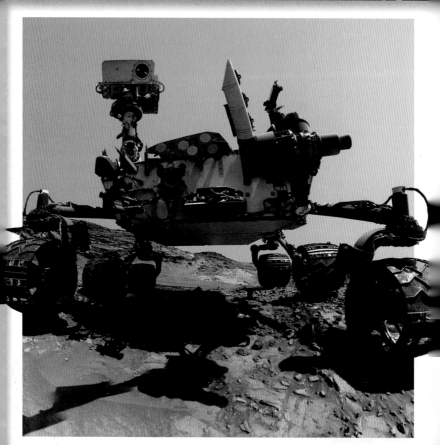

CURIOSITY **TAKES SOME AMAZING SELFIES**

The Mars rover has a long camera arm that stretches out so that it can photograph itself. It then transmits the photos home to Earth.

PLAY IT!

...e your rover and astronauts ...ars! It's a whole new world of ...enture. What will they find on ...Red Planet? Will they be safe?

Meet the *Curiosity* rover. In 2011, this robot vehicle was rocketed off to Mars. Since 2012, it has been on its own Mars adventure. It snoops around, taking photos and sending information back all the time. *Curiosity* has not bumped into any Martians yet, but it is always looking for signs of life.

So far, *Curiosity* has made some useful discoveries. It has drilled down into the rock and found that there might have been life on Mars millions of years ago. It has tested the air to see if it would be safe for humans to visit. Scientists now think that there is water on Mars. Will *Curiosity* explore it? And even find living creatures? We can't wait to find out!

Curiosity is woken up every Mars day with a song from Earth!

Breaking news! Water on Mars, 30 miles (48 km) from Curiosity. Read all about it!

Umm, Curiosity travels only 2 metres a minute!

I'd better get MY skates on . . . !

Play it! Here are some ideas . . .

1 *Do your astronauts have a rover to ride on?*

2 *If you dig under the surface, what will you find?*

3 *Do aliens live on Mars?*

Lift off

It takes a lot of power to blast a spacecraft into space. The spacecraft is attached to a huge rocket that has to be super powerful to get itself off the ground.

Soyuz
The *Soyuz* rocket can take three astronauts into space. It takes off from Kazakhstan, in Asia. There are four stages of lift-off.

STAGE THREE

About five minutes after take off, a large section of the rocket falls off. The rocket is now 105 miles (169 km) high.

STAGE TWO

After about two minutes, the rocket drops the four boosters to the ground. It is about 25 miles (40 km) up in the sky.

STAGE ONE

Lift off! The four boosters blast the rocket into the air.

SUPER SPEED

The rocket travels at 25,000 miles per hour (40,200 kph)!

Build it!
Build a rocket in three sections: spacecraft, engines, boosters.

STAGE FOUR

After nine minutes, the last engine is dropped and the spacecraft is free. It is about 140 miles (225 km) high, and in space.

ASTRONAUTS

The astronauts are in a small capsule inside this section. They can't see out until stage four.

He also said that suddenly going into zero gravity is like being thrown off a cliff. Gulp!

Oooof, yes, that's exactly what it feels like.

3, 2, 1 . . . whoooaaa! The Canadian astronaut Chris Hadfield flew three space missions. He said that take off feels like having a big gorilla sitting on you.

Blast off!

Check out these strange things that have been blasted off Earth and carried into space!

Fruit flies

Let's go!

3, 2, 1 . .

Blast off!

MINIFIGURES

Three special LEGO® minifigures are travelling to Jupiter right now!

LIGHTSABER

Luke Skywalker's lightsaber from the Star Wars movies flew into space.

SANDWICH

A naughty astronaut once smuggled up a corned-beef sandwich!

In 1960, Strelka the dog flew into space. She later had six puppies. One of the pups was given to the president of the United States.

White mouse

MOON TREES

In 1971, 500 tree seeds were taken to the Moon and back. They were all planted on Earth and are known as "Moon trees."

"Jingle Bells" on a harmonica was the first song to be played in space.

SPACE TOURIST
Richard Garriott paid $30 million to spend ten days on the ISS.

DINOSAUR
A Coelophysis skull travelled on the space shuttle Endeavour.

CHIMPANZEE
Ham the chimp was sent into space and returned safely.

TORCH
The Olympic torch went into space, but it was too dangerous to light it!

The ISS astronauts played football in space to celebrate the 2014 World Cup. Hey! Where'd the ball go?

Octan

Space-walk adventure

ASTRONAUTS BUILDING THE ISS

These photographs show brave astronauts
space walking. They are building and mending
the ISS ... while wearing huge gloves!

PLAY IT!
Now build your own
astronauts and send them on
space-walk adventures!

Building a lab in outer space

The International Space Station (ISS) is an enormous science lab, as big as a football pitch. It orbits Earth about 200 miles (322 km) up in space, moving at about 17,500 miles per hour (28,200 kph). But how did it get up there?

Building it was a real space adventure! It was rocketed up in thousands of pieces. Then astronauts had to build it. Building began in 1998, and astronauts are still adding and mending parts. The astronauts have to put on huge space-suits, then climb out of the space station to work on it. They are attached by ropes so they don't float away. They have to be expert builders as well as astronauts!

Ok, put on those gloves and get out there . . . We need a new toilet.

But I can barely hold this spanner! These gloves are ENORMOUS!

The longest space walk was 8 hours and 56 minutes, so we'd better get going. I think I need the bathroom!

Play it! Now invent your own . . .

 1 *What are your astronauts building in space?*

 2 *Is there any chance they will float away?*

 3 *What can they see from space?*

The space-suits that astronauts wear on space walks are like mini spaceships. Everything that an astronaut needs to live is built into the suit – even the toilet!

GLOVES

Gloves have heated fingertips to keep hands warm.

Hot or cold?
It is really, really cold in space. But if the Sun is shining on you, it's burning hot. Space suits protect from the cold and the heat.

NAPPY

Astronauts wear super-thick underwear so that they don't have to return to the space station to go to the bathroom!

Camera

Air tank

HELMET

A helmet is very strong, to protect the astronaut's head if anything flying by hits it.

"SNOOPY CAP"

Under the helmet, the astronaut wears a cap with headphones and a microphone built in.

DRINKING BAG

There is a straw near the astronaut's mouth for sipping water during a space walk.

Ooh, I love your gold helmet visor. It's so blingy!

It's not bling, it's useful. It's gold to protect my face from the Sun's dangerous rays.

The ISS

Up to ten astronauts live on the International Space Station (ISS) at one time. Each stays for about six months. Life is very strange on the ISS.

> She has even wilder hair than I do!

Delivery!
All the food has to be delivered to the ISS by spacecraft. The *Progress* spacecraft flies without anyone on it and locks onto the ISS.

Zero gravity
There is no gravity on the ISS, so food floats away and hair stands on end. Even water floats away in bubbles!

Sleep well!
Astronauts have to strap themselves to the walls when they sleep. Otherwise, they float around and bump into things.

A cheese and salami pizza was once delivered to the ISS. It travelled at over 16,000 miles per hour (25,700 kph). Now that's fast food!

Build it!

Your astronauts need a space base. Design a space station. Here are some of the important parts.

Solar panels

Living quarters

Docking station

Viewing window

Laboratory

Radiator

GIANT RUBBISH BIN

The astronauts send the *Progress* spacecraft away with all their rubbish!

Space lettuce

Astronauts are trying to grow food in space. They recently grew some salad greens. It was the first food grown away from Earth!

Build it bigger!

Now that you've made your space station, build a delivery probe that can attach to it. Something needs to take out the rubbish!

SCOTT KELLY ON THE ISS

Floating fruit nearly drove Scott Kelly bananas on the ISS. But at least the views of Earth were great from the space station.

PLAY IT!
What adventures will your astronauts have on your ISS?

The next big step in space travel is to rocket a person to Mars. But will that make human bones turn to jelly? Or brains go squishy? It's time to test a human. In March 2015, astronaut Scott Kelly was one of two space travellers blasted off Earth to spend a whole year on the ISS. No other American has spent as much time in space as Scott has! His body was tested from top to bottom.

During that year, Scott exercised for over 700 hours. He drank 730 litres of his own recycled urine and sweat . . . yuck! He also did about 383 tests on his body. Scott has an identical twin brother here on Earth who was tested, too, to compare how their bodies behaved. Mars, here we come!

So if we drink our wee and sweat, what happens to astronaut poo?

Well, actually, it burns up in our atmosphere and becomes shooting stars.

Are you telling me that the next time I make a wish on a shooting star, I'll be wishing on astronaut poo?

Play it! Here are some ideas . . .

 Do they feel strange floating around?

 Will they spot other spaceships?

 What happens if an alien arrives?

39

The asteroid belt

Asteroids are rocks that orbit the Sun. There are millions of asteroids that float around between Mars and Jupiter. This ring of rocks is known as the asteroid belt.

KLEOPATRA

The asteroid Kleopatra looks like a dog's bone!

Ragged rocks

Asteroids can be 6 metres to 500 miles (805 km) across! They come in lots of different shapes. None of them is completely round.

Most people think that the dinosaurs were wiped out because a big space rock hit Earth.

That's not such a bad thing . . . Arrgh!

Gold rush! I've heard that there's an asteroid filled with gold. People are already racing to mine it. It's mine!

HAYABUSA

The space probe is about the size of a car.

Touchdown

The Japanese space probe *Hayabusa* left Earth in 2003 to visit the asteroid Itokawa. It took samples of the soil and brought them back to Earth in 2010.

Most asteroids that race towards the Earth are burned up into tiny pieces in our atmosphere. The ones that get through are called meteorites.

Jupiter

Jupiter is the king of the planets in our solar system. It's so big that all seven other planets could fit inside it!

Gas giant

Jupiter is the gas planet nearest to the Sun. It is a giant ball of gas and liquid. If you flew to Jupiter, there would be no place to land!

LIGHTNING

Super-bolts of lightning on Jupiter are much more powerful than most flashes on Earth.

Juno

The space probe *Juno* is on its way to Jupiter. It's going to take a peep through the thick clouds for the first time.

> Jupiter is the biggest planet, the fastest-spinning planet and the planet with the biggest moon. It's a record breaker. I know how it feels!

Jupiter's moons

Jupiter has 67 moons (spotted so far!). And 4 of the rocky moons are huge! Io is covered in volcanoes and is constantly spewing sulphur into space.

PLANET STATS

- Made of: Gas
- Moons: 67
- Rings: 3
- Distance from Sun: 484 million miles (779 million km)
- Space-probe missions: 9

The weather on Jupiter is windy and wild, and storms can last for hundreds of years. Let's fly by.

What will Juno find? A humongous hurricane? A flaming fireball? Daggerlike ice rain?

Do you mind?

We're playing Snap.

43

Saturn would float in water if there was a bathtub big enough!

Saturn

Saturn is not as big as Jupiter, but it's still an ENORMOUS ball of gas. It is the most spectacular planet because of the amazing rings around it.

The rings

Saturn has seven rings. Each one is made of billions of pieces of ice. Some pieces are the size of sand grains; others are the size of buses.

Sigh. So beautiful . . .

Not me!

Saturn's sky

The space probe *Cassini* has been poking around Saturn's moons. There are some pretty strange ones.

Mimas

Mimas has a huge crater on it that makes it look like an eyeball!

Tethys

Tethys looks like someone has scribbled across it with red crayon.

PLANET STATS

- Made of: Gas
- Moons: 62
  - Rings: 7
  - Distance from Sun: 886 million miles (1.4 billion km)
- Space probe missions: 5

GIANT DISKS

The rings are only about half a mile (0.8 km) thick – but 24,000 miles (38,600 km) wide!

Half and half!

Brr! Does this melt?

Come and visit soon

Iapetus

One side is completely black and the other side is

Enceladus

Enceladus is a huge ocean covered in a layer of ice

Titan

Titan is very similar to Earth. Could it have life on it?

Uranus and

PLANET STATS

- Made of: Gas and liquid, with rock in the centre
- Moons: 27
- Rings: 13
- Distance from Sun: 1.8 billion miles (2.9 billion km)
- Space-probe missions: 1

Uranus and Neptune are far, far away. They are very dark, very cold and super stormy.

URANUS

Uranus has rocky rings around it — but they are not as impressive as Saturn's.

Blue twins

Balls of gas with rocky centres. Methane gas makes them blue. Uranus is the only planet that spins tilted, on its side.

I can deal with the cold, but I'm worried about the smell. They are GASSY planets, after all . . . poooh!

Neptune

PLANET STATS

- Made of: Gas and liquid, with rock in the centre
- Moons: 14
- Rings: 6
- Distance from Sun: 2.8 billion miles (4.5 billion km)
- Space-probe missions: 1

NEPTUNE

Neptune has the most violent weather in the solar system. Its storms are ten times stronger than Earth hurricanes.

VOYAGER 2

It took the space probe 12 years to reach Neptune!

Voyager 2

In 1977, *Voyager 2* flew into space. It stopped off at Uranus and Neptune to have a look around.

Scientists think that Uranus may have liquid diamond oceans with diamond icebergs . . .

Oh, that is just too much sparkle! TAKE ME THERE!

Hmm, the sparkle may whip around your head at 700 miles per hour (1,100 kph) . . .

Give me your helmet then.

Sigh . . . Those silly Earthlings strike again.

In 1977, the *Voyager 1* space probe was launched. Like its twin, *Voyager 2*, it was sent to explore nearby planets, but *Voyager 1* went far beyond. It is now at the edge of the solar system.

FAR, FAR AWAY

Voyager 1 is now over 12 billion miles (19 billion km) away. It's the man-made object the furthest away from Earth.

The aliens will love the Golden Record, especially the music.

I'm sure they'll love all that Bach and Beethoven.

What? No disco?

1980 – Flies by Saturn, 886 million miles (1.4 billion km) away

1977 – Launches from Earth

1979 – Flies by Jupiter, 484 million miles (779 million km) away

2015 – Reaches the edge of the solar system, 12 billion miles (19 billion km) away

The Golden Record

The probe is carrying a golden disc holding photographs, music, animal sounds and messages from Earth. It is so that aliens can find out what life on Earth is like.

Scientists think there might be a giant planet - Planet X - at the edge of our Solar System. Perhaps Voyager I will spot it.

ANTENNA

The antenna lets *Voyager I* talk to Earth.

SPEEDY

The probe travels 870,000 miles (1,400,000 km) a day.

INSTRUMENTS

Voyager I is covered in very clever instruments that measure things like temperature. It's pretty chilly out there!

Pluto's moon, Charon

Travel beyond Neptune and you'll reach a ring called the Kuiper Belt. There are millions of icy objects here. Some of these are round. They are known as dwarf planets.

Planet no more

Pluto was once one of the main planets. Then, in 2006, scientists changed their minds and called it a dwarf planet instead. Poor Pluto.

Headline news! Some scientists think that Pluto should be turned BACK into a main planet again. Make up your minds!

The New Horizons probe travels 1 million miles (1.6 million km) a day.

PLUTO

New pictures show that Pluto is covered with mountain ranges, deep valleys and red and orange patches!

New Horizons

In 2015, the space probe New Horizons sent back the first close-up images of Pluto. No aliens have been spotted . . . yet!

ARRGH! A monster with two eyes!

ARRGH! A monster with one eye!

Comet adventure

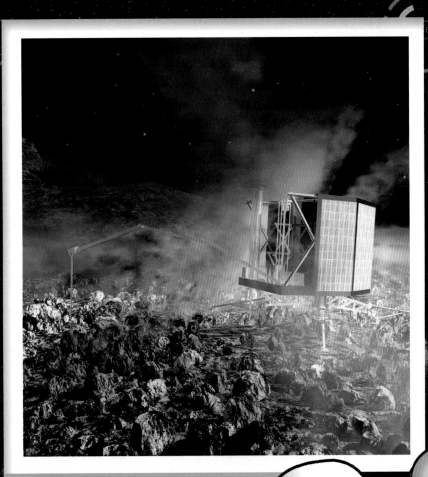

ROSETTA'S LANDER ON THE COMET

After setting down on the comet, the lander quickly started working. Then it went quiet. Several months later it sprang back into life and sent more data.

PLAY IT!
Send your rock-star astronauts out to find and follow a comet! Comets are super speedy, so it will be tricky to catch one!

Chasing rocking rocks!

A comet is a chunk of icy rock that often starts off in the Kuiper Belt. Then it suddenly gets a push from another rock and is hurled towards the Sun. Comets leave icy tails behind them. They can sometimes be seen shooting across the sky from Earth.

In 2004, a space probe called Rosetta was sent out to chase a comet and land on it. After an epic ten-year journey, Rosetta reached a comet. It sent a small lander down onto the comet. The comet was travelling at 34,000 miles per hour (55,000 kph), so it was a tricky move!

Rosetta discovered that the 2-mile-wide (3.2 km) comet is so light that it would float on water. It also sniffed the comet and found that it smells of rotten eggs, horse stables and marzipan. EW!

When I asked you if you wanted to see some epic rock, I meant comet-watching . . .

No worries. Comets are cool. I hear that they may have metal in them, too . . .

Rock AND heavy metal! Awesome!

Play it! Here are some ideas . . .

1 What will your astronauts travel in?

2 What will they be singing as they arrive?

3 What is the comet made of? Heavy metal?

Exoplanets

In 5 billion years' time, the Sun will begin to die. NO Sun = NO life! Don't panic. Astronomers have discovered many other stars in our galaxy that also have planets. These planets are known as exoplanets. Time to move!

Kepler space telescope

Kepler, a huge telescope, stares at the same patch of sky all the time. It has spotted over 1,000 exoplanets so far.

Kepler

There could be 160 billion exoplanets out there in the Milky Way. We've got some serious house hunting to do!

I can't wait to see our new home! Are we there yet? Are we there yet?

Home away from home

Gliese 832 c has a similar temperature to Earth's, though its sun is not as bright as ours. It could also have water on it. BUT, big problem – it would take us 400,000 years to get to it!

GLIESE 832 C

Kepler is always looking for Earth's twin planet. Gliese 832 c is the planet most similar to Earth that has been found so far.

Do you think we'll find water or flowers or houses or chocolate?

Nope, looks like we're all alone. Except for that big grey guy . . . !

New home

Could someone rename these planets to something a bit more catchy . . . like Dave or Marge?

There are lots of mega-strange exoplanets that no one would ever want to live on!

OGLE-2005-BLG-390L b
You'll need your skates to get around on this icy planet. It's the coldest planet ever found. Brrrr.

55 Cancri e
This planet is thought to be made of diamonds. And it's eight times the size of Earth. Bling it on!

Wow, there are some crazy worlds out there!

WASP-12 b

This super-hot exoplanet orbits its star so closely that the star is eating it. It has only 10 million years left before it's swallowed whole!

GJ 1214 b

This planet might be nothing but a hot, giant ocean. That's one huge, scorching hot tub!

TrES-2 b

This planet has no light at all. It is seriously dark. Nobody knows why. It just is.

PSO J318.5-22

This planet has no sun! It just drifts around in space with nowhere to go. No sunrises or sunsets – that's too sad.

Far, far away

What will we spot next? The Hubble Space Telescope has already discovered some amazing things. The brand-new James Webb Space Telescope, launching in 2018, is much more powerful than Hubble!

Hubble Space Telescope
Hubble is a telescope that orbits Earth. It has photographed galaxies. It has even spotted two crashing into each other.

Galaxies crashing

Hubble Space Telescope

The star closest to our Sun, Proxima Centauri, is 24,800,000,000,000 miles (39,900,000,000,000 km) away.

Hmm, I could do with my nearest neighbour being that far away . . .

Morning, Bob. Can I read your paper when you finish?

Black holes

Hubble has detected strange things in space called black holes. A black hole is a star that is dying and sucking everything around it into a hole, like water down a drain. It even sucks up light!

If you were sucked into a black hole, your body would stretch. You'd look like this pretzel!

beep erp zig zama

z*rp zepo

Alien life

Are we alone in space? Nobody knows, but scientists are doing their best to find out if there is more life out there. What would an alien look like, if we met one?

WATER BEARS

These tiny Earth creatures can live in space – with no space-suits! Perhaps aliens look like this!

59

What's next?

Hotel Moon
Don't book your holiday for 2025 yet. You may be able to visit a Moon hotel!

First on Mars
Jump on the Orion spacecraft, and you may be the first to step on Mars!

MISSION: ASTEROID
Next stop — send humans to an asteroid. Then capture it and drag it back to Earth!

My perfect summer job. I get to cook food, serve it, and chase it! I'm over the Moon!

Our future in space

Holidays in space

Sleep travel

Humans on Mars

Space elevator to ISS

Lassoing asteroids

Skin-tight space suits

Super-powerful James Webb Space Telescope

Glossary

asteroid
A small rocky object that travels around the Sun.

atmosphere
The blanket of gasses that surrounds a planet.

black hole
A dying star that has such strong gravity that it even pulls light into it.

comet
A small, icy object that travels towards and away from the Sun. It does not move in a perfect circle around it.

constellation
A group of stars that form a pattern that can be recognized.

crater
A hole in the ground of a planet caused by a large rock crashing into it.

dwarf planet
A small planet that travels with other groups of rocks around the Sun.

exoplanet
A planet that orbits another star outside our solar system.

galaxy
A group of billions of stars that are held together by gravity and move together in space.

gravity
A force that pulls objects towards it, a bit like a magnet. Earth's gravity stops us from floating away.

lander
A spacecraft that can land on the surface of a space object such as a planet, moon or comet.

moon
An object that moves around, or orbits, a planet.

My space adventure may be over, but I can't wait to hear about what else is out there!

> Come and find us, Earthlings! We're out here waiting!

orbit
The journey that a space object takes when it moves around another object in space.

planet
A round object that moves around a star.

rover
A moving vehicle that explores a planet or other object in space.

solar system
A star and everything that travels around it, such as planets and rocks.

space probe
A vehicle that is sent into space to explore and send back information to Earth.

sun
The star that our Earth travels around. It gives us warmth and light.

visor
Part of a space helmet that can be moved down to cover the face.

Build it!
Build an incredible space station for a faraway planet. What will your minifigures need to survive?

Houses

Restaurant

Supermarket

Cinema

Swimming pool

Laboratory

Build it bigger!
Now build a giant alien space station! What strange buildings might the aliens have?

Index and credits

Index

Photo credits

For the LEGO Group: Randi Kirsten Sørensen *Assistant Manager*, Peter Moorby *Licensing Coordinator*, Heidi K. Jensen *Licensing Manager*, Paul Hansford *Creative Publishing Manager*, Martin Leighton Lindhardt *Publishing Graphic Designer*.
Photographs ©: cover space background: ESA and A. Nota (STScI/ESA)/NASA; cover centre top planet: NASA; cover bottom left planet: NASA; cover bottom right planets: PHL @ UPR Arecibo (phl. upr.edu), ESA/Hubble/NASA; cover top left: JPL/Space Science Institute/NASA; back cover bottom left: Andrey Armyagov/Shutterstock, Inc.; back cover bottom right: NASA; back cover top left: NASA; 1 background: NASA; 2 background: NASA; 2 centre right: JPL-Caltech/NASA; 4-5 space background and throughout: NASA; 4-5 centre: Ken Thornsley/iStockphoto; 6 centre left Earth: pkproject/iStockphoto; 6 bottom left: ClaudioVentrella/iStockphoto; 6 bottom centre: WorkinghamOwl/iStockphoto; 6 bottom right background: ESA/Hubble/D. A Gouliermis/NASA; 6 bottom right Hubble Space Telescope: NASA; 6-7 top rocket: 3DSculptor/iStockphoto; 7 all other images: NASA; 7 right centre left: JPL/NASA; 7 right bottom right: Ames Research Centre/NASA; 8 centre right: NASA; 8-9 background: SDO/NASA; 10 sun and planet: Detlev van Ravensway/
Science Source; 11 top centre: Detlev van Ravensway/Science Source; 11 centre planets: Detlev van Ravensway/Science Source; 12 bottom left: Johns Hopkins University Applied Physics Laboratory/Carnegie Institution of Washington/NASA; 12-13 Mercury: Johns Hopkins University/APL/NASA; 13 top left Earth and throughout: pkproject/Shutterstock, Inc.; 13 bottom left top: Michael Carroll/Alien Volcanoes by Lopes and Carroll, The Johns Hopkins University Press, 2008/NASA; 13 bottom left bottom: Johns Hopkins University Applied Physics Laboratory/Carnegie Institution of Washington/NASA; 13 centre asteroid: JPL-Caltech/UCAL/MPS/DLR/IDA/NASA; 13 top left Mercury: Johns Hopkins University/APL/NASA; 14 bottom thermometer: digitalgenetics/iStockphoto; 14-15 all other images: NASA; 16 centre left bird: Benny Rytter/iStockphoto; 16 top centre rocket: Boeing Images/NASA; 16 bottom right lion: Eric Isselee/iStockphoto; 16-17 Earth background: USGS/NASA; 17 top left butterflies: thawats/iStockphoto; 17 centre right Earth: Karsten Schneider/Science Source; 18-19 all other images: NASA; 19 top left Earth: USGS/NASA; 20 centre: NASA; 20 top left, 20 top right and throughout: clusterx/Fotolia; 20-21 background and throughout: ESO/Serge Brunier, Frederic Tapissier/NASA; 22 bottom centre: yganko/iStockphoto;
22 bottom right: yganko/iStockphoto; 22 bottom left: Kgkarolina/iStockphoto; 23 top sky: Son Gallery - Wilson Lee/Getty Images; 23 bottom right: yganko/iStockphoto; 23 bottom centre: AlexanderZam/iStockphoto; 23 bottom left: rendixalextian/iStockphoto; 24-25 Mars: Stocktrek Images/Getty Images; 25 centre right moon: JPL-Caltech/University of Arizona/NASA; 25 centre left moon: G. Neukum (FU Berlin), Mars Express, DLR, ESA/NASA; 26 centre: JPL-Caltech/MSSS/NASA; 28-29 main: Joel Kowsky/NASA; 30 top left flies: Antagain/iStockphoto; 30 centre bottom right: DebbiSmirnoff/iStockphoto; 30 centre bottom left: Neil Lockhart/Shutterstock, Inc.; 30 bottom left: fotofermer/iStockphoto; 30 bottom right: Antagain/iStockphoto; 30 centre top right: Francois Gohier/Science Source; 30 centre top left: LEGO/JPL-Caltech/KSC/NASA; 31 top centre: Dmitry Lovetsky/AP Images; 31 top right: NASA; 31 bottom left: Marc Tielemans/Alamy Images; 31 bottom right soccerball: Samuray/iStockphoto; 31 centre right spiders: Jeffrey Schreier/iStockphoto; 31 top left: Francois Gohier/Science Source; 32-33 all images: NASA; 34-35 main: Andrey Armyagov/Shutterstock, Inc.; 36-37 all images: NASA; 38 all images: NASA; 40 all other asteroids: Science Photo
All LEGO illustrations and stickers by Paul Lee and Sean Wang.

That was far out! Let's go home to Earth.